Frank Mundell

The Man who Freed the Slaves

The Story of Abraham Lincoln

Frank Mundell

The Man who Freed the Slaves
The Story of Abraham Lincoln

ISBN/EAN: 9783744794893

Printed in Europe, USA, Canada, Australia, Japan

Cover: Foto ©ninafisch / pixelio.de

More available books at **www.hansebooks.com**

THE MAN WHO FREED THE SLAVES

THE STORY OF ABRAHAM LINCOLN

BY

FRANK MUNDELL

AUTHOR OF "CAPTAIN COOK" "JAMES A. GARFIELD" ETC.

*WITH ILLUSTRATION IN COLOUR BY
JOHN CAMPBELL*

PUBLISHED AT 57 AND 59 LUDGATE HILL, E.C.

BY THE SUNDAY SCHOOL UNION, LONDON

CONTENTS

THE MAN WHO
FREED THE SLAVES

———◆———

CHAPTER I.

INTRODUCTORY.

FOR nearly three hundred years after the discovery of America the interior of the country remained practically unknown. Beyond the Alleghany Mountains all was wilderness, hostile savages, and wild beasts. Gradually, however, as fresh arrivals came into the settlements the older colonists began to feel themselves, "crowded," as they said, so, packing up their belongings, they set off westward to seek some spot where they could "breathe."

These hardy pioneers did much to open up the interior of the North American continent—more perhaps than any amount of organised exploration could have accomplished.

One part of the country thus opened up was Kentucky, and thither in 1780 came one Abraham Lincoln. He was of English stock, being descended from Samuel Lincoln, who in 1638 had emigrated from England and settled in Massachusetts. He, however, before long fell a victim to the hostility of the Indians, being killed while peacefully at work on his farm. His youngest son, Thomas by name, became thus "a wandering, labouring boy," and grew up without even the rudiments of an education. As he reached manhood he learned something of carpentering in the shop of Joseph Hanks of Elizabethtown.

When he reached the age of twenty-eight, Thomas Lincoln married Nancy Hanks, a niece of his employer. She is described as a good-looking young woman of twenty-three, and was so far superior in education to her husband that she could read and write. She taught him to sign his name. Mrs. Lincoln seems strangely out of place amid the rude surroundings of pioneer life. She was small, slender, and sensitive, of a nature that shrank instinctively from the wild, rough life around her; but she was a woman of a winning manner, and a nature as true as it was gentle. Her son ever regarded her memory with the fondest affection, and long after, when he had left all association with those early days far behind, he paid a glowing tribute to her worth. "All that I am or hope to be," he said, "I owe to my angel mother; blessings on her memory."

Thomas Lincoln, more in keeping with his surroundings, better adapted to bear with them, was less fitted to battle with them. He was one of those easy-going, good-natured souls who are content to take life as they find it, and who, rather than make an effort at any improvement either in themselves or their condition, are content to jog along from day to day, with the dubious consolation that things might be worse. He was a favourite with every one; but he was sadly lacking in those qualities of energy and purpose necessary at all times, but doubly so in a new land where the very needs of life have to be won from the soil.

A year after his marriage, Thomas Lincoln moved to a small farm on the Big South Fork of Nolin Creek. He got the place cheap, but it was an unfortunate speculation, for the ground was rocky, barren, and weedy. Here, on the 12th of February 1809, Abraham Lincoln was born. A few years later, Thomas Lincoln took another farm not far distant, and the family remained there till Abraham was seven years old. Little, indeed nothing, is known of those early years, but we can infer that poverty and hardship played no small part.

New settlers began to come into the region, and the inborn restlessness of Thomas Lincoln began to assert itself, and soon he decided to strike westward in search of land and " room." He therefore sold his farm to some new arrivals for ten barrels of whisky and £4 in money, and set off to have a look at the new territory of Indiana, about which he had heard glowing accounts. He built a little flat boat, and launched it on the Rolling Fork, a tributary of the Ohio. Having loaded with some of the heavier of his household goods, he pushed off and floated down to the junction of the rivers. Here, however, his frail craft was upset, and most of his belongings went to the bottom. With the few things he managed to save he landed at a place called Thomson's Ferry. Thence he struck across country for about eighteen miles, till he reached Spencer County, Indiana, where in an almost unbroken wilderness he determined to make his home.

Leaving his goods in care of a settler, he went back for his family. The journey to the new home was made overland, upon three horses, which carried in packs the bedding, clothing, and personal belongings. The distance was about fifty miles, but the nature of the country and the lack of roads made it considerably longer. Having accomplished the journey safely, the family took up their abode in the new home—a spot about two miles east of what afterwards became the town of Gentryville.

It was now late in the autumn of 1816, and the first care of the father was to provide some kind of shelter for his wife and children. He hastily knocked together a rude shanty. It was enclosed on three sides, and open to the weather in front. Here the fire was made to save building a chimney. As a summer residence it left little to be desired; but it afforded most inadequate protection against the rigour of winter. Here, however, they spent the first twelve months of their sojourn in Indiana. It must not on this account be thought that Thomas Lincoln was lazy or neglectful. He was busy on the land from early till late, for there was much to be done, and the future was of more consequence than the present. Trees had to be cut down, a fence erected to enclose the farm, and the land had to be prepared for the crop on which their future food entirely depended.

As soon as time permitted he erected a cabin. Of course everything was of the rudest description, but it was all their own, and the future was theirs, and with hopeful hearts they looked forward to better days. Before these days were to dawn, however, a deeper shadow fell on the little household. The mother's health broke down under the cares and privations, and within two years after her removal to Indiana she died, and was laid to rest under the trees near the cabin.

To Abraham the loss of his mother was a terrible blow. Child as he was, he remembered how, as he sat at her feet, she would cheer the long winter evenings with stories of her own early days, and tales which she as a girl had listened to and read—tales of adventure, daring, hardship, and heroism, mingled with stories of endurance, suffering, and duty. As he sat by the simple mound that marked her last resting-place, he thought of it all, and there came to him another thought, that it was at least fitting there should be some kind of religious service held over one whose life had been a prayer for others. He spoke to his father, and between them they made up a letter to Parson Elkin in Kentucky. It was a rude epistle. Abraham's penmanship had been acquired from a brief and casual school attendance, but there was enough of it to convey the desired message.

It was no small thing to ask the good parson to come fully a hundred miles through the wilderness to preach the funeral sermon over one so humble as the wife of a pioneer settler, and it speaks volumes for the man that he replied that he would come, and also fixed the day. Notice was promptly given to all the country round, and at the appointed time people came from far and near to be present. Some came in carts with the huge boles of forest trees for wheels, others in ox-waggons, some two on a horse, some on foot, so that when Parson Elkin stood up he had before him an audience of two hundred persons.

"The occasion, the eager faces round him, and all the sweet influences of the morning inspired him with an unusual fluency and fervour, and the flickering sunlight as it glanced through the wind-parted leaves caught many a tear on the bronzed cheeks of his listeners, while father and son were overcome by the revival of their first great grief. He spoke of her who had gone with the warm praise she deserved, and held her up as an example of true womanhood."

CHAPTER II.

Making a Start.

A LITTLE more than a year after, Thomas Lincoln decided to marry again, and brought to his home a widow with three children.

She was fortunately a woman of energy and decision, and with these qualities she combined the rarest of all attributes—a heart. Her coming was a blessing to the husband—to the orphan children it was a mercy. She brought many things for the home, and one of her first acts was to provide the neglected little ones with clothing and comforts. To them she seemed almost like some fairy godmother. She seemed to infuse new life and vigour into all about her. Under her energetic management the cabin was made habitable. A floor was made, doors and windows were fitted, and for the first time in his life Abraham began to have some idea what it was to have a home. Throughout his life he never ceased to remember with feelings of the

utmost gratitude the many kindnesses he owed
to her generous heart.

And she, quick to discover the sterling nature
of the boy, sought to encourage and help him by
every means in her power. All the schooling
he had had was of the most meagre and broken
description,but it was enough to give him a
start on the pathway of knowledge, especially
when he was so eager to learn. He read every
book he could lay his hands on, and it was his
habit, when he came across a passage that
struck him as being in any way noteworthy, to
write it down. If he had no paper, he wrote it
on boards, and kept it by him till he got paper.
Then he would re-write it, study it, repeat it.
He used to put all these jottings in a kind of
scrap-book, and so preserved them for future
use and reference.

It goes without saying that the choice of
books in the wilderness was not extensive ; but
what was lacking in quantity was more than
made up for in quality. The favourite volumes
were *Robinson Crusoe, Æsop's Fables*, Bunyan's
Pilgrim's Progress, and a *Life of Washington*.
It must not be thought that Abraham read, as
so many do, to kill time and annihilate thought.
He read with all his senses on the alert that
he might penetrate beyond the words to their

meaning, and beyond the book to its message. He sought for, and rarely failed to find, a lesson.

An instance of this, all the more remarkable for its being furnished by himself many years afterwards, is well worth recording. Alluding in one of his speeches to the *Life of Washington* just mentioned, he said—

" I remember all the accounts there given of the battlefields and the struggles for the liberties of the country, and none fixed themselves upon my imagination so deeply as the struggle here at Trenton, New Jersey. I recollect thinking then, boy though I was, that there must have been something more than common that these men struggled for."

Little did he then dream that his own name was destined to stand in the history of his country as second only to that of his hero, as the saviour of his country and the liberator of a race.

It must not be forgotten that Lincoln's efforts at self-education were not sudden, spasmodic, or brief. Indeed, on the contrary, they extended over a period of thirteen years, and during this time he was working hard for a living. Perseverance so unflinching could not but have its reward. When we remember that from the time he was old enough to hold an axe till he was twenty-three years of age, the tool was little out of his hands; when we remember the mental apathy brought about by severe and long-borne physical toil, we are struck by the consciousness of abundant intellectual power, and the lofty purpose of the lad, who could thus look forward to the day, yet afar off, when his laboriously acquired lore should stand him in good stead in forwarding his career.

When he was eighteen years, old Lincoln got the idea that it would be a good thing to take the produce of the farm down the river to a market. Of course the first necessity was a boat, but that offered no insurmountable obstacles to one familiar as he was with the use of tools. Of the voyage and its results we have no knowledge; but before starting an incident occurred which made a pleasant and lasting impression on his memory, and was in the nature of a good omen.

As he was about to set off, two men came down the bank and asked Lincoln to row them out to a steamer that was coming down the river. He agreed, and put them on board. Just as he shoved off he was surprised and pleased by two silver half-dollars falling into the boat, as payment for his services. In afterwards speaking of this incident, Lincoln remarked—

"You may think it was a very little thing, but it was a most important incident in my life. I could scarcely believe my eyes. I could scarcely believe that I, a poor boy, had earned a dollar in less than a day. The world seemed fairer and wider before me. I was a more hopeful and confident being from that time."

In the following year he had another and more extended river experience, and on this occasion was rewarded with his first glimpse of the outside world. He was engaged by the owner of a neighbouring store to accompany his son in charge of a boatload of produce to New Orleans. For this service he was to receive eight dollars a month and his board. Lincoln eagerly embraced the chance of earning so much, especially as the trip promised him a chance of seeing something of what was going on in the busy haunts of men.

On this trip he had an adventure which might easily have cost him his life. Arriving at a sugar plantation, the boat was pulled inshore, and tied to the bank for the night. Some time after he had fallen asleep he was aroused by a noise. "Who's there?" he called. He received no answer. Suspecting that something was amiss, he sprang to his feet, and saw several negroes coming stealthily forward. Guessing their object at once, he seized a handspike and knocked the first man that came on board into the water. Three more who followed were served in the same fashion.

Standing on the bank, the others seemed to be discussing their future course of action. Before they could come to any decision, however, they saw Lincoln coming towards them with long and rapid strides. They promptly turned and fled, but he followed and overtook them, and gave each a sound drubbing. Such was Lincoln's first acquaintance with the race for which he afterwards gave his life.

New Orleans was reached without further incident worthy of remark. Having disposed of the cargo, the boat was broken up and the voyagers set out for home. One of them at least carried back with him an indelible picture. He had become acquainted for the first time with slavery, and had witnessed it in all its misery, wretchedness, and degradation. The picture was truly one to harrow the feelings and make the flesh creep, one that needed to be seen but once to remain in the memory for ever like some hideous nightmare. There is no record of what Lincoln thought of these unaccustomed scenes, but we can hardly doubt that the picture of misery he looked on then came back to him in later years, to stir his heart and nerve his brain amid the fury of the strife he waged that the black man might be free.

Working thus for others, receiving but the humblest wages, reading, studying in the all too brief intervals of toil, helping his father on the farm, picking up scraps of information from new-comers and neighbours, and earning the goodwill of every one with whom he came in contact, the thirteen years of his life in Indiana wore away.

" With a constitution as firm and flexible as whipcord, he had arrived at his majority. The most that could be said of his education was that he could read and write and count. He knew nothing of English grammar, he could not read a sentence in any tongue but his own: all that he knew, however, he knew thoroughly. It had all been assimilated, and was part not only of his possessions but of himself. While acquiring, he had learned to construct, organise, and express. There was no part of his knowledge that was not an element of his practical power. He had not been made by any artificial process, he had grown. Holding within himself the germ of a great life, he had reached out his roots like the trees among which he was reared, and drawn to himself such nutriment as the soil afforded. His individuality was developed and nurtured by the process. And this was the secret of all his subsequent success. He succeeded because he had himself and all his resources completely in hand, for he was not and never became an educated man in the general sense of the term."

His moral character was beyond reproach. As one admirer puts it—" No stimulant ever entered his lips, no profanity ever came from them." He was a capital story-teller, and, under all circumstances, good-natured. His honesty and truthfulness were proverbial, and he was as popular throughout the region where he lived as he afterwards became throughout the nation.

CHAPTER III.

THE LOCAL CHAMPION.

FOR some time Thomas Lincoln had been growing more and more dissatisfied with his farm. The region was unhealthy and the land unproductive. Nothing could be got out of it without great labour and heavy expense. From time to time he heard glowing accounts of the rich prairie lands of Illinois. There, it was said, were almost boundless farms within easy reach of wood and water, with soil so fertile as to require nothing but the plough and the hoe to make them immediately productive. During all the years he had toiled he had never been able to do more than provide for the wants of his household, and now he thought it was time to make a move to some more favoured spot.

Accordingly he sold his claim in Indiana, and on the 1st of March 1830 started for the land of promise, accompanied by his wife and family. The journey was difficult, and tedious in the extreme. The rivers were swollen by the melting of the snow, and the spring rains made the tracks heavy for the ox-teams that pulled the waggons loaded with the entire worldly possessions of the settlers.

A journey of fifteen days brought them to Macon county. Here they halted, and Thomas Lincoln, having selected a piece of land, prepared to settle down again. Abraham helped his father to build a log-cabin and to get the home in order; then he split rails for a fence and helped to enclose ten acres. After breaking up the ground and seeing the corn planted, he told his father that he intended to go away from home and seek his fortune.

He accordingly became a labourer, ready and willing to do a day's work for a day's pay for anybody anywhere. He split rails to get clothing, and with one settler he made a bargain to split four hundred rails for every yard of brown jeans dyed with white walnut bark that would be needed to make him a pair of trousers. In those days he thought nothing of walking five or six miles to his work.

A man who occasionally worked with Lincoln at this time describes him as the roughest looking person he ever saw. He was tall, angular and ungainly, and wore trousers made

2

of flax and tow, cut tight at the ankle and out at the knee.   Though known to be very poor, he was a welcome guest in every house for miles round.

During the winter of the great snow, when no other work was to be had, Lincoln and two others arranged with a trader named Denton Offutt to take a boatload of provisions to New Orleans. When the time came for them to make a start, it was found impossible to procure a boat.   Nothing daunted, they offered to build him one, and finally an arrangement was come to by which he agreed to pay them twelve dollars a month each.

It took some time to get the timber and build the boat, and when it was finished the river had fallen so low that the new craft stuck midway across a mill dam at New Salem, with its bow in the air and its stern under water. Here was a pretty fix.   Such a thing had never been seen or heard of before, and those who saw the mishap called to their neighbours to come and see the boat that couldn't float and hadn't made up its mind to fly.

Numerous were the witticisms passed at the expense of the luckless voyagers ; but Lincoln was equal to the occasion, and turned their laughter into admiration by a device as novel as it was simple.   He bored a hole in the bottom of the boat at the bow, and rigged up a kind of rude derrick to lift the stern, so that the water she had taken in behind ran out in front. In this way he managed to float the boat over the partly submerged dam, to the no small amazement and delight of the spectators, who never in all their experience had seen any one make a boat float by boring a hole in it.

Offutt was so well pleased with Lincoln, that he proposed he should go to New Salem to look after a mill and a store he had there. The men he had hitherto employed had not only cheated him, but had driven away custom by their careless habits, and this made him doubly anxious to secure the services of one whose honesty and ability were alike beyond question. Abraham was ready for anything that might come along, and gladly closed with the offer. So he became a "clerk," as they say, in a grocery store.

He had none of the airs and graces of the shopman of civilisation, but for all that he worked up the business and attended to it as no one had done before. All the old customers came back, new ones were gained, and the shrewd trader had reason to congratulate himself on his choice.

Several incidents connected with this period of Lincoln's history are well worth narrating for the light they throw on his character. One evening a woman came into the store and made some purchases, for which she paid. On adding up the bill afterwards he found that he had made a slight overcharge. It only amounted to a few pence, but as far as he was concerned these pence might as well have been pounds. The moment he had closed the shop he set out for the woman's house, three miles away, and gave her the money.

On another occasion, just at shutting-up time, a woman came in for half a pound of tea. Lincoln served her, and immediately afterwards shut the shop. Next morning he found a four-ounce weight in the scales, and his mistake of the night before immediately flashed across his mind. Then and there he weighed out another four ounces, and without waiting to get his breakfast he set off to deliver the remainder of the tea.

These are in themselves very humble incidents indeed, but they are of great importance, for they illustrate Lincoln's perfect conscientiousness and sensitive honesty better than if important matters and larger amounts had been in question. Little wonder is it that

here he got the name that clung to him
through life—"Honest Abe."

Another incident which occurred at this
time shows, better perhaps than any other,
the great spirit that animated him. One day,
while several women were in the store, a
well-known bully came in. From the first
it was evident he was in search of trouble.
He shouted, used bad language, and talked
generally in a most offensive manner. Lincoln
leaned over the counter, and asked him, as
there were ladies present, to put some restraint on his language. To this mild protest
the bully replied that he would do as he
liked, say what he had a mind to, when and
where he pleased, and he should jolly well
like to see the man that objected.

Lincoln calmly answered that if he would
be good enough to wait till the ladies retired,
he would listen to all he had to say, and
would take great pleasure in giving him all
the satisfaction he could desire. As soon as
the women left the shop the man became
furious. He felt he had been publicly humili-
ated, and the knowledge was like fuel to fire.
Lincoln listened for a while in silence, but
seeing nothing would satisfy the fellow but
a fight, he said quietly, "Well, if you must

be thrashed, I suppose I may as well do it as any other man. Come along outside."

Out of doors they went. The battle that followed was short and decisive. Without any trouble Lincoln threw his man, and held him down with one hand, while with the other he plucked some smartweed that grew near. With this he rubbed the bully's face till he roared again. When the job was finished, he went for water, washed the bully's face, and did all in his power to undo the damage he had done.

It was at this period of his career that Lincoln began the study of English grammar. There was not a text-book to be obtained in the neighbourhood, but, happening to hear of a man eight miles off who possessed a copy, he walked to the house and succeeded in borrowing it. A lawyer who used frequently to visit New Salem tells how, every time he visited the town, Lincoln used to ask him to explain some point in the book that had given him trouble. When he had mastered the book, he remarked, " Well, if that's what they call a science, I think I can subdue another."

Every minute that could rightfully be spared from business Lincoln spent in the pursuit

The Local Champion 23

of knowledge. One snapshot we have of him
at this time is well worth framing. A friend
who called on him one day found him lying
on a trundle bed covered with books and
papers, and rocking a cradle with his foot.
He explained simply that he was looking
after the baby, while the mother was busy
attending to some pressing household matters.

Lincoln remained with Offutt for a year,
when the business failed and Lincoln found
himself "out of work." As he looked back on
these twelve months he saw much reason to
congratulate himself on the general progress
he had made. It had been a noteworthy
year in other respects. He had read many
books, and he had mastered English grammar.
He had also won a multitude of friends.

" Those who could appreciate brains respected
him—those who were devotees of muscle were
devoted to him—every one trusted him. He
was judge, arbitrator, referee, umpire and
authority in all disputes and games, in matches
of men and horses. He was a peacemaker in
all quarrels, everybody's friend, the best-natured,
most sensible, the best-informed, the most
modest and unassuming, the kindest, gentlest,
roughest, strongest, best young fellow in all
New Salem and the region round about."

CHAPTER IV.

AN OFFICIAL APPOINTMENT.

ABOUT this time the Indians gave the Government some cause for anxiety. A chief named Black Hawk, in defiance of the treaty made with his tribe, crossed from the western bank of the Mississippi with the avowed intention of regaining the old hunting grounds of his people on the eastern side of the great river. When ordered to go back he returned a defiant answer, and continued on his way at the head of his tribe.

As they would not return peaceably, it became necessary to drive them back by force of arms. Volunteers were therefore called for, and among the first to enlist was Abraham Lincoln. Many of the men were from his part of the country, and when the time came to choose a captain the unanimous choice of the soldiers fell on Lincoln.

No subsequent success in life, he used to say, had ever given him half the satisfaction that this election did.   It was the first public recognition of merit he had received, and to one who had laboured so strenuously and in face ot difficulties and disadvantages so formidable, the distinction meant much.   He was a most popular officer, because he was thoroughly familiar with the ways and modes of thought of the men he had to handle, and did not make the somewhat natural mistake of treating them as soldiers.

The Black Hawk war was really an affair of little moment, and fizzled out in much the same insignificant fashion as it began.   Lincoln merely regarded it as an episode in his career.   Only once afterwards did he refer to his part in the campaign, and then merely for the purpose of turning to ridicule the pretensions of an opponent.   He was at the time a representative in Congress, and General Cass was a candidate for the Presidency.   Hoping to win him the popular favour, his friends sought to endow him with a martial reputation; but Lincoln turned these pretensions to ridicule in a speech that was highly humorous and bristling with sarcasm.

" By the way, Mr. Speaker," he said, " do you know I am a military hero ?   Yes, sir !   In the days of the Black Hawk war I fought, bled, and came away. Speaking of the career of General Cass reminds me of my own. If he went in advance of me in picking whortleberries, I guess I surpassed him in charges on the wild onions. If he saw any live fighting Indians, it was more than I did; but I had a good many sanguinary struggles with the mosquitoes, and though I never fainted from loss of blood, I can truly say I was often very hungry."

When the soldiers returned home they found that the State election would take place in ten days, and though the time was so short Lincoln was asked to allow his name to be put up as a candidate for the Legislature, as the American State Parliament is called. The request came as a great surprise to him, for he was young—only twenty-three years of age—and had not any of the advantages possessed by his opponents. He however allowed himself to be nominated, but the time at his disposal was too short to permit him to become generally known, and he suffered his first and last defeat, as he was wont to say, at the hands of the people.

Lincoln was now, in a sense, at the parting of the ways. He was without means and without employment; but not for long. A nature so energetic does not wait for something to turn up, but instead goes out and turns something up. He put his hand to any work he could get. For a while he assisted the surveyor of the county, and then he was given what he humorously called an official appointment—he was appointed postmaster at New Salem. It was given him for two reasons—first, that every one liked him and wanted to see him get on ; and second, because he was the only person who could and would trouble to make out the necessary official returns. The appointment was grateful to him for another reason, because it gave him an opportunity of reading every newspaper that came into the neighbourhood.

The post had one drawback—that it kept him tied to the office rather more than he cared about; but this trifling difficulty he got rid of in a way peculiarly his own. He transformed himself into a perambulating post office, and whenever he wished to go out he placed the letters in his hat. When any one expected a letter, all he had to do was to ascertain the whereabouts of the postmaster. "When he found him he found the office, and the public officer taking off his hat looked over the mail wherever the public might find him."

It was during his connection with the post office that one of the most splendid instances of

Lincoln's rigid honesty came to light. He had passed through a period of great poverty and hardship, he had studied law, and in the course of this he had been subjected to many inconveniences and perplexities, sufficient in the opinion of many to have warranted him making a temporary use of any money that happened to be in his control. One day an agent called to close the post office accounts, and informed the postmaster that there was a balance due from him to the department.

A look of perplexity crossed Lincoln's face. The friends who were with him at the time saw it, and naturally enough concluded that he was in a difficulty. "Abe, let us help you if you are in want of money," said one.

He answered nothing ; going to a corner, he pulled out a little old trunk and brought it to the table. "What does the balance amount to ?" he asked. The sum was named. Thereupon he opened the trunk, pulled out a little package of coin wrapped round with a piece of rag, and counted out the exact sum the official had named—amounting to about seventeen dollars. After the agent had left, Lincoln quietly remarked, as if in answer to the thoughts of his friends, that he never used any man's money but his own. During all the time the money had been in his hands he had never once thought of using it to relieve his own wants even for the moment.

His next appointment was that of assistant to the surveyor of Sagamon county. He knew nothing of the work, but with characteristic thoroughness he set about getting a working knowledge of his duties. From his chief he borrowed some books on the subject, and after a brief period of study he turned out a full-fledged surveyor, with compass and chain. This work was most welcome; it provided him with the necessaries of life, and enabled him to indulge a little in his favoured luxury —books. For over a year Lincoln was employed on the survey, and so well did he understand his business, and so accurately did he carry it through, that his surveys have never been found inaccurate.

CHAPTER V.

A New Sphere.

THE year 1834 saw Lincoln once more a candidate for the Legislature, and on this occasion he was returned by the highest number of votes ever polled by one candidate. There was also elected Major Stuart, an officer whom Lincoln had known in the Black Hawk war. Stuart, who was engaged as a lawyer in Springfield, had a great admiration for the abilities of his stalwart friend, and, like every one else, was only too anxious to help him. He offered to lend Lincoln the books required to study law, an offer which it is almost needless to say was accepted with gratitude.

Lincoln set to work with the utmost enthusiasm. He studied while he had bread, and then set out on a surveying expedition to win the money that would buy more. It soon became evident that he had found his life work. So overpowering was his earnestness, that people thought he had gone demented. Day after day, for weeks, he would go and sit under a tree on a hill near New Salem and read, moving round the trunk as the sun moved to keep in the shade. So absorbed was he that he would pass his friends in the street without even a nod of recognition.

When the time for the assembling of the Legislature drew near, Lincoln abandoned the law, shouldered his pack, and on foot travelled the hundred miles to Yandalia, the capital, to make his entry into public life. His first session was uneventful. He said little, but he learned much. When the business came to an end he returned home, as he had come, to his law books and his surveying. In the autumn of 1836 he was admitted to the bar, and in the following spring he removed from New Salem and took up his quarters at Springfield, the new capital, to start a legal partnership with his friend Stuart.

" The time had come with Lincoln for translation to a new sphere of life. By the scantiest means he had wrested from the hardest circumstances a development of his natural powers. He had acquired the rudiments of an English education. He had read several text-books of the natural sciences ; he had read law as well as he could without the help of teachers. He had attended a few sessions of the courts held near him, and had become somewhat familiar with the practical application of legal processes. He had from the most discouraging beginnings grown to be a notable political debater."

In 1840 he was again elected. In the same year his partnership with Stuart was dissolved, and he joined Judge Logan, one of the ablest and most learned lawyers in the State. It had been his intention to devote rather more of his time to business than to politics, but the people had learned too well his worth and would not do without his services.

Two years later, having reached his thirty-third year, he married Mary Todd, a daughter of the Hon. Robert S. Todd of Lexington, Kentucky. His domestic arrangements were of the simplest kind, as may be seen from a letter written to a friend, in which he says, " We are not keeping house, but boarding at the Globe Tavern, which is very well kept."

During the next few years Lincoln devoted all his energies to the work of his profession. Many are the characteristic stories belonging to this period, but we must content ourselves with a few of the more striking examples of his honesty, kindness, and love of impartial justice. It is said that he never made his profession pay, and we cannot wonder at it. It was almost impossible for him to charge a heavy fee to any one, and if his client happened also to be his friend, it was still more impossible to make any charge at all. To those poor and in needy circumstances he was more apt to give than to take.

One day an old woman of seventy-five came tottering into his office to lay her grievance before him. She was the widow, she said, of one of the men who had fought for his country's freedom at the Revolution, and her trouble was that an agent had charged her two hundred dollars for collecting the pension money. With a promise to look into the matter and let her know the result, he sent the old woman away. He at once set to work to make inquiries, and finding the woman's story true, he entered a suit against the agent to force him to disgorge a portion at least of his plunder.

Lincoln's address to the jury was long remembered for its beauty and pathos. After referring in a few stirring sentences to the period of the Revolutionary war, how every man was needed, and how gallantly every man responded to the call to arms, he pictured the hardships of the campaign, and how, in recognition of their services, the country had pensioned those who fought her battles. In tones of withering scorn, he referred to the agent who did not scruple to rob this poor lonely old woman of her all. Long before he had finished speaking there was hardly a dry eye in the court, and the jury unanimously gave him the verdict. The old woman recovered a hundred dollars, and went back to her home rejoicing.

Another case is well worth recording, bearing as it does on the great life-work of our hero. An old negro woman called upon him once in sore distress. She and her children were born slaves in Kentucky, and her master had brought them all into Illinois and given them their freedom. Her son had gone down the Mississippi as one of the crew of a steamboat, and on arriving at New Orleans had imprudently gone ashore. In accordance with the law then in force, he was taken into custody, and subsequently ordered to pay a fine.

The boat had meanwhile left, and, having neither friends nor money, he was in danger of being sold to pay the fine and expenses. Lincoln was greatly moved by the story, and sent over to the State House to ask if anything could be done to get the negro back. The reply he received was that nothing could be done. Boiling with wrath, he rose to his feet and declared that if he didn't get the negro back soon there would be a twenty years' agitation in Illinois till the Government obtained the right to do something under such circumstances. It is satisfactory to know that Lincoln and his partner sent money of their own to New Orleans and procured the man's release.

Some of Lincoln's cases turned on points altogether remote from law. A young man named Armstrong, whom Lincoln had known in his early days, was charged with having killed a man during the progress of a row. Honest Abe" was asked to defend him ; and, having assured himself of his client's innocence, he agreed to take up the case. The prosecution had to all appearances an impregnable case, and their witnesses were numerous. When they had all had their say, Lincoln stood up. The principal witness had sworn that " by the aid ot the brightly shining moon he saw the prisoner inflict the death-blow." He called for an almanac, and, turning to the date in question, proved beyond all dispute that there was no moon that night. His client was of course at once acquitted.

Throughout his career, Lincoln gave many proofs of his fearless regard for truth and justice, but few so unmistakably convincing as the following.

A sheep-grower sold a number of sheep at a certain average price. When he delivered the animals, it was found that there were among them a number of lambs, or sheep too young to come within the meaning of the contract. The buyer sued for damages, and Lincoln defended. At the trial it came out that all sheep under a certain age were by custom regarded as lambs and of a less value. When Lincoln heard this, his whole attitude changed, and instead of the brilliant cross-examination the court expected, he simply asked the number of inferior sheep actually delivered. Then, turning to the jury, he told them that on the evidence they must give a verdict against his client.

But we must leave these anecdotes, pleasant and instructive though they be, for we are now approaching the greatest epoch in Lincoln's history, and indeed one of the grandest in the world's story.

CHAPTER VI.

THE CHAMPION OF FREEDOM.

AMID the busy life of his profession, Lincoln still found time to keep himself in touch with politics. That a great constitutional movement was in process of development he never had any doubt, though in what form or to what end it should show itself it was impossible to forecast. In 1854, the new political era opened. Two new territories—Kansas and Nebraska—had been admitted to the Union, and a deliberate attempt was made to force slavery on them. "Popular sovereignty" was the specious title of this new idea, and the leading motive of it was the absolute right of the people of a territory to decide their own institutions for themselves. No mention was made of slavery, but it was clear to all but the wilfully blind what the promoters of the movement had in mind.

Lincoln saw clearly the outcome of this manœuvre, and the political iniquity of the whole business roused him as nothing before had ever done. He began to see that there never could be an abiding peace on the question till it was finally and for ever settled for or against slavery. In this, as in other things, he felt that half measures would foster rather than heal the sore. With all his marvellous power and energy he set himself to denounce the new doctrine that had crept into the State. As he said on one occasion, " Slavery, according to our opponents, is right. Slavery is entitled to equal consideration with freedom. Slavery claims the privilege of going wherever into the national domain it may choose to go. Slavery claims national protection everywhere. Instead of remaining contented with the territory it occupied under the protection of the Constitution, it is seeking to extend itself indefinitely, to nationalise itself."

Lincoln was desperately in earnest, and he never missed an opportunity of attacking the Bill. Even its supporters felt that a man of strength was its enemy, and that if strong and manly efforts could defeat it, it would be defeated. At a meeting at Springfield he put the whole matter clearly before his audience.

" The supporters of the Bill say it is an insult to the emigrants to Kansas and Nebraska to suppose that they are not able to govern themselves. We must not slur over an argument of this kind because it happens to tickle the ear. It must be met and answered. I admit that the emigrant to Kansas and Nebraska is competent to govern himself, but— I deny his right to govern any other person without that person's consent."

As time wore on, slavery was rapidly raised from the narrow limits of party politics and became a burning national question. Lincoln was recognised as its foremost and most powerful opponent. His hatred of the institution was intense, and he was united with a party whose avowed purpose was to restrict it to those parts of the country where it held its only rights under the Constitution. It was largely through his help that the Republican party in Illinois was organised. Wherever he went his eloquence electrified the audience, and all the Western Republicans regarded him as their first man. They accordingly presented his name to the National Convention as their candidate for the Vice-Presidency. The vote, however, went against him, but the nomination served as his formal introduction to the nation.

At one of the meetings of this campaign an incident occurred that is worthy of being recorded. When he had finished speaking, one of the audience asked—

"Mr. Lincoln, is it true that you entered this State barefoot, driving a yoke of oxen?"

Lincoln paused for a full half-minute, as if considering whether or not he should take notice of such brutal impertinence.

"Yes," he said at length, "and I think I can prove the fact by at least a dozen men in this company, any of whom is more respectable than my questioner." The crowd cheered him to the echo, and as soon as quiet was again restored he went on to show what free institutions had done for him, and asked his audience if it was not natural that he who had benefited so much by free institutions should hate slavery and agitate against it. "Yes," he continued, "we will speak for freedom and against slavery as long as the Constitution of our country guarantees free speech, until everywhere on this wide land the sun shall shine, and the rain shall fall, and the wind shall blow upon no man who goes forth to unrequited toil."

This may be almost regarded as his dedication of himself to the cause of the slave. Henceforth his life was absorbed by politics to the exclusion of all other interests. He took his stand in this great question not on any party basis or personal consideration, but on the surest of sure foundations—the Declaration of

Independence. How closely he had reasoned the whole matter is shown in a speech which he delivered about this time. Referring to the nation's charter of liberty, he said—and his words are a lucid and convincing exposition of the true meaning of the immortal Declaration—

"The thirteen colonies, by their representatives in old Independence Hall, said to the world of men, 'We hold these truths to be self-evident, that all men are born equal, that they are endowed by their Creator with inalienable rights ; that amongst these are life, liberty, and the pursuit of happiness.' This was their majestic interpretation of the economy of the universe. This was their lofty, wise, and noble understanding of the justice of the Creator to His creatures. Yes, gentlemen, to all His creatures, to the whole great family of man.

"In their enlightened belief, nothing stamped with the Divine image and likeness was sent into the world to be trodden on and degraded and imbruted by its fellows. They grasped not only the race of men then living, but they reached forward and seized upon the farthest posterity. They created a beacon to guide their children, and their children's children, and the countless myriads who should inhabit the earth in other ages.

" Wise statesmen as they were, they knew the tendency of prosperity to breed tyrants, and so they established these great self-evident truths, that when in the distant future some man, some faction, some interest should set up the doctrine that none but rich men, or none but white men, or none but Anglo-Saxon white men, were entitled to life, liberty, and the pursuit of happiness, their posterity might look up again to the Declaration of Independence, and take courage to renew the battle which their fathers began, so that truth and justice, mercy, and all the humane and Christian virtues, might not be extinguished from the land, so that no man would hereafter dare to limit and circumscribe the great principles on which the Temple of Liberty was being built.

" Now, my countrymen, you have been taught doctrines conflicting with the great landmarks of the Declaration of Independence, if you would listen to suggestions that would take away from its grandeur or mutilate the fair symmetry of its proportions. If you have been inclined to believe that all men are not created equal in those inalienable rights enumerated by our charter of liberty, let me entreat you to come back, return to the fountain whose waters spring close by the blood of the Revolution.

Think nothing of me, take no thought of the political fate of any man whomsoever, but come back to the truths that are in the Declaration of Independence.

"You may do anything with me you choose, if you will but heed these sacred principles. You may not only defeat me for the Senate, but you may take me and put me to death. While pretending no indifference to earthly honours, I do claim to be actuated in this contest by something higher than an anxiety for office. I charge you to drop every paltry and insignificant thought for any man's success. It is nothing, I am nothing. But do not destroy that immortal emblem of humanity, the Declaration of American Independence."

He was chosen to oppose Judge Douglas, whose term of office was expiring, and the speech he made before the convention that nominated him bristled with good points. He told his hearers that the question of slavery must be settled once and for all. "A house divided against itself cannot stand," he warned them. "I believe this Government cannot endure permanently half slave and half free. I do not expect the Union to be dissolved. I do not expect the house to fall—but I do expect it will cease to be divided. It will become all one thing or all the other. Either the opponents of slavery will arrest the spread of it and place it where the public mind shall rest in the belief that it is in course of extinction; or its advocates will push it forward till it shall become alike lawful in all the States—old as well as new, North as well as South. The result is not doubtful. We shall not fail—if we stand firm, we shall not fail. Wise counsels may accelerate or mistakes delay it, but sooner or later the victory is bound to come."

Lincoln went throughout the length and breadth of the State, meeting everywhere with unbounded enthusiasm; but when election day came the vote went against him. Asked by a friend how he felt on his defeat, he replied, with characteristic humour, that he felt like the boy who had bruised his toe—too badly to laugh, and too big to cry. Though defeated, he did not regard himself as a beaten man, nor was he so regarded; and when he entered the hall at the Illinois State Republican Convention on the 10th of May, he received an ovation such as is never accorded but to successful men. There could be no mistaking the high honour and warm affection with which he was regarded, and it was equally plain that his nominal defeat was regarded as no less than the prelude of a grand triumph whose fruits would not be long delayed.

As he journeyed eastward, Lincoln became somewhat oppressed by the thought of speaking before eastern audiences. It was one thing to address the people who knew and understood him, but it was an entirely different matter to appear before audiences who from long habit had come to expect their politicians to be also orators. But his fears were groundless. His clear-cut and incisive words and the thorough knowledge he possessed of his subject carried far more weight than any flowery periods of oratory. Those who heard him could not withhold their admiration, esteem, and applause.

It was on the 25th of February 1860 that he made his appearance before a New York audience. "He began his address," says one who was present, "in a low, monotonous tone, but gaining confidence in the respectful stillness, his voice rose in strength and gained in clearness, until every ear heard every word. His style of speech was so fresh, his mode of statement was so simple, his illustrations were so quaint and peculiar, that the audience eagerly drank in every sentence. The backwoods orator had found one of the most appreciative audiences he had ever addressed, and the audience gave abundant testimony they were listening to the utterances of a master."

Wherever he went it was a repetition of his triumph. He spoke at several places in New England and before immense audiences, over whom he exerted a power and influence that seemed nothing short of miraculous. A visit to Harvard University brought his tour to an end. As he was saying "Good-bye" to his many new-found friends, the Rev. John P. Gulliver of Norwich said—

"You have become one of our leaders in this great struggle with slavery, which is undoubtedly the great struggle of the nation and the age. What I would like to say to you is this, and I say it with a full heart, 'Be true to your principles, and we will be true to you, and God will be true to us all.'"

Touched by his earnestness, Lincoln replied, "I say Amen to that! Amen to that!"

CHAPTER VII.

THE PATH OF SAFETY.

LINCOLN brought back with him from his Eastern tour the pleasantest recollections. He had seen much and learned much, and all went to prove that the difference between East and West was not so great as he had imagined. He found that the people in the East judged a man by much the same standard as did the folks out West—by what he is, and by what he can do. Of all men, Lincoln had little to dread in standing up before the world under these conditions.

Events meanwhile were shaping men's minds insensibly for the coming struggle. The slavery-supporting South was manifestly determined not to brook the slightest interference with slavery, and her only remaining hope was to secede from the Union. Indeed, she but waited a favourable moment to throw down the gauntlet. Her supporters everywhere—and she had many in the North—were, secretly but none the less vigorously, working in her cause; her arsenals were being filled with munitions of war, and men were being prepared to bear arms. Her counsellors had anticipated everything, prepared for everything—all that was wanted was a fitting opportunity and a valid cause of war.

On the 17th of June 1860, the Republican party met at Chicago to nominate their candidate for the Presidency. On the same day in the little city of Springfield, two hundred miles away from the excitement and furore, sat Lincoln, waiting for the news on which depended his fate as a public man and his place in history. The results of the convention would be momentous to him and to the nation. He foresaw, if no one else did, the nature of the great struggle to which his nomination and election were but the prelude.

He put on his hat and went up to the *Journal* office to hear how things were going. There he met several of his friends, all, like himself, in a state of tremendous excitement. At length a telegraph messenger arrived and handed to Lincoln the long-waited missive, at the same time announcing to those in the room that their friend had been adopted as the Republican candidate. When the congratulations were over, Lincoln put the telegram in his pocket, and remarking that there was a little woman on

Eighth Street who would like to know the good news, went home.

And thus, election following nomination, Abraham Lincoln became President of the great Republic in the fifty-second year of his age. He had achieved this lofty position—a position we may almost say of sovereignty—by sheer force of character, and in face of as forbidding difficulties and threatening impossibilities as ever beset a man who sought to raise himself above his circumstances. How would he acquit himself? How would he carry the country through the peril which was looming large on the political horizon? Time alone should tell; but if indications were not altogether worthless, the nation had chosen the man for the hour.

The news of Lincoln's election filled the Southern States with anger and dismay. They knew his determined attitude towards slavery; they knew his unflinching virtue; they knew he was not to be turned from his purpose by any personal considerations. He was not the man for them. No! they would not be dominated by such a man. They would resist to the uttermost; they would leave the Union; if need be, they would fight.

The spirit in which Lincoln approached the

4

difficult problem is in marked contrast to this passionate outburst. In his first inaugural address as President he said—

"It is exceedingly desirable that all parts of this great confederacy shall be at peace and in harmony one with another. Let us Republicans do our part to have it so. Even though much provoked, let us do nothing through passion and ill-temper. Even though the Southern people will not so much as listen to us, let us calmly consider their demands, and yield to them if in our deliberate view of our duty we possibly can.

"If our sense of duty forbids us to allow slavery to spread into the Territories, then let us stand by our duty fearlessly and effectively. Let us be diverted by none of those sophistical contrivances wherewith we are so industriously plied and belaboured — contrivances such as groping for some middle ground between the right and the wrong, vain as the search for a man who should be neither a living nor a dead man ; such as a policy of 'Don't care' on a question about which all true men do care ; such as Union appeals beseeching all true men to yield to disunion ; reversing the Divine rule, and calling not the sinners but the righteous to repentance ; such as invocations to Washington imploring men to unsay what Washington said and undo what Washington did.

"Neither let us be slandered from our duty by false accusations against us, nor frightened from it by menaces of destruction to the Government nor of dungeons to ourselves. Let us have faith that right makes might, and in that faith let us to the end do our duty as we understand it."

Conciliatory and indeed appealing as his words were, there was in them nothing of fear; they are the firm expression of an unanswerable case, having stated which, he goes on to speak of the future in words no less certain.

" In doing our duty there need be no bloodshed or violence, and there need be none unless it be forced upon the national authority. The power confided to me will be used to hold, occupy, and possess the property and places belonging to the Government, and to collect the duties and imposts ; but beyond what is necessary for these objects there will be no invasion, no using of force against or among the people anywhere.

" The course here indicated will be followed, unless current events and experience shall show a modification or change to be proper; and in every case my best discretion will be exercised according to circumstances actually existing, and with a view and a hope of a peaceful solution of the national troubles and the restoration of fraternal sympathies and affections."

Dealing with the threat of the South to leave the Union, Lincoln said, "The central idea of secession is the essence of anarchy. A majority held in restraint by constitutional checks and limitations, and always changing easily with deliberate changes of popular opinions and sentiments, is the only true sovereign of a free people. Whoever rejects it does of necessity fly to anarchy or to despotism. Unanimity is impossible ; the rule of a minority as a permanent arrangement is wholly inadmissible, so that, rejecting the majority principle, anarchy or despotism in some form is all that is left.

"Physically speaking, we cannot separate. We cannot remove our respective sections from each other, nor build an impassable wall between them. The different parts of our country cannot but remain face to face, and intercourse either amiable or hostile must continue between them. It is impossible, therefore, to make that intercourse more advantageous or more satisfactory after separation than before. Can aliens make treaties easier than friends can make laws? Can treaties be more faithfully enforced among aliens than laws among friends?

"Suppose you go to war, you cannot fight always; and when, after much loss on both sides and no gain on either, you cease fighting, the identical old questions are again upon you.

"My countrymen one and all, think calmly and well upon this whole subject. Nothing valuable can be lost by taking time. Intelligence, patriotism and Christianity, and a firm reliance on Him who has never yet forsaken this favoured land, are still competent to adjust in the best way all our present difficulty.

"In your hands, my dissatisfied fellow-countrymen, and not in mine, is the momentous issue of Civil War. The Government will not assail you. You can have no conflict without being yourselves the aggressors. You have no oath registered in heaven to destroy the Government, while I shall have the most solemn one to preserve, protect, and defend it.

"I am loath to close. We are not enemies but friends. We must not be enemies. Though passion may have strained, it must not break our bonds of affection. The mystic cords of memory stretching from every battlefield and patriot grave to every living heart and hearthstone all over this broad land will yet swell the chorus of the Union when again touched, as surely they will be, by the better angels of our nature."

Lincoln's path was one not merely of difficulty but of danger. On his way to Washington to take up the duties of his high office, he had to proceed by unexpected and unusual routes, for his enemies had sworn he should not reach the Capitol alive. On his arrival he was coldly received. His enemies were so numerous and so powerful, that his friends were in fear of exasperating them to some rash iniquity. Amid it all he was calm, unruffled, and to all appearances unconscious of the untoward conditions. On afterwards being asked if he felt at all frightened while delivering his address, he replied that he had frequently experienced greater fear in saying a few words to some of the men out West on the subject of temperance.

Because he joked thus, it must not be thought he was ignorant of or indifferent to the true state of affairs in the administrative capital of the country. Treason was rampant everywhere and in every department of the public service. The Government was betrayed daily, and many times a day. Resolutely Lincoln adhered to the course he had indicated. By no appearance of hostility would he precipitate the catastrophe which threatened; on no account would he be the first to open fire.

Meanwhile the South carried out their threat of secession. South Carolina, Georgia, Alabama, Florida, Mississippi, Louisiana, and Texas left the Union and formed themselves into "The Confederate States of America," with Jefferson Davis as their first President. They seized all the forts, arsenals, and public buildings within their limits, and bade defiance to the North. Lincoln had told them that they could not have a conflict without being themselves the aggressors, and they had taken him at his word —a conflict they would have. For years they had been preparing for it, and they were all in readiness to strike, and to strike hard.

Their first move was to attack Fort Sumter at Charlestown. They laid siege to it, but it defied their best efforts. They were not, however, to be denied, and, after sustaining a thirty-four hours' bombardment, the garrison was forced to surrender on the 13th of April 1861.

Thus opened the Civil War. No longer could even the most sanguine look for any settlement of the vexed question of slavery other than the stern arbitrament of arms.

The North bounded from its long restraint with patriotic eagerness, burning to wipe out the stain on their beloved flag and hurl back the insult to the Union. "Better it should be settled by us than by our children," said men everywhere.

Lincoln, forbearing, conciliatory, peace-loving as he had been, showed himself no laggard in face of the national danger. He had been most unwilling to strike a blow, but when the blow had been struck he was no craven to dally in returning it. By proclamation he called for 75,000 men at once, and a few weeks later ordered a further enlistment of 65,000 soldiers and 18,000 sailors for three years' service. He further instituted a blockade of the Southern ports, and took active steps to organise a navy. A special session of Congress was convened, and he asked for powers to make the war "short, sharp, and decisive." With enthusiastic readiness the country responded to his every wish.

Nor were the people of the South one whit less enthusiastic, and four additional slave States that had hitherto held aloof threw in their lot with their neighbours.

Such were the preliminaries of "one of the most remarkable wars that have occurred in the history of the human race—a war which, for the number of men involved, the amount of space traversed, of coast-line blockaded, of material consumed and results achieved, surpasses all the wars of history."

CHAPTER VIII.

WAR.

THE South was quick to follow up the advantage they had gained. Troops were pushed northward with feverish haste. Their public men were already boasting that the war would not be fought on Southern ground, and that their flag would soon wave triumphant over the Capitol at Washington. That they had been long preparing for war was evident, and now they seemed about to reap the fruit of their cuteness. The North, on the other hand, had everything to do and no time to do it in. Heedless of these considerations, the people looked for immediate results, and were indignant that they were not forthcoming. To satisfy their clamour more than for any other reason, the battle of Bull Run was fought, and resulted in the flight of the Northern soldiers. It might easily have resulted in something much more serious, for it left Washington at the mercy of the invaders. Fortunately for the North, fortunately for humanity, the Confederates did not know how easily they might have turned a success into a triumph.

The result of this engagement was a great blow to Lincoln. With the penetration of the true statesman, he saw how much his cause had lost by this precipitate action; all hope of a peaceful solution to the question that vexed them was indefinitely postponed. He, however, found great comfort in the readiness Congress displayed to strengthen his hands and to spare nothing in the cause of humanity and right. He asked for *four* hundred million dollars to carry on the war—they gave him five hundred millions; he asked for 400,000 men—they gave him leave to raise half a million.

In a few short months he had a magnificent army in the field. Again his hopes were blighted and his expectations brought to nothing. Weeks passed, spent for the most part by the commander in making excuses why he had not done one thing and finding obstacles that would prevent him doing another. At one time he had not enough men, at another not enough stores. Everything that could be done was done to meet his demands, and he was urged again and again to immediate action; but the summer passed, the autumn came and went, and still he was preparing to strike the blow that was never struck, even if it ever was intended to be made.

The new year, 1862, opened well. Forts Henry and Donelson fell before General Grant, who also won the battle of Shiloh. Roanoke Island was seized by Burnside, who captured 3000 prisoners. Farragut ran his fleet past the forts of Jackson and St. Philippe and forced the surrender of New Orleans. This was a most important victory, for it enabled the Federals to gain control of the Lower Mississippi. This period also witnessed the famous fight between the ironclads *Monitor* and *Merrimac*, which ended in the Confederate vessel being destroyed. The most notable event of this period was the surprise of the Northern soldiers under General Grant at Pittsburg Landing. The rebels attacked them in overwhelming numbers on the 6th of April, and drove them back. On the following day, however, the Federals were reinforced, and, attacking once more, forced the enemy to retreat.

The high hopes roused by these successes were doomed to early disappointment. For the next three months disaster followed disaster. The campaign against Richmond failed. Pope's army advancing against the same city by another route was beaten and had to fall back on Washington. The fortune of war turned to the North again in the defeat of Lee's invading army at South Mountain and Antietam.

So well was Lincoln pleased with the progress of events so far, that we find him writing: " Peace does not appear so far distant as it did. I hope it will soon come, and come to stay, and so come as to be worth the keeping in all future time. It will then have been proved that among freemen there can be no successful appeal from the ballot to the bullet, and that they who make such appeal are sure to lose the case and pay the cost."

With varying fortune the war went on. After the defeat at Chancellorsville, when 18,000 men perished, General Lee led the Southern troops into Maryland and Pennsylvania. The whole country became terribly alarmed. Lincoln called for 100,000 men to drive back the invaders, and General Meade went forth to do the work. On the 1st of July the armies met at Gettysburg in Pennsylvania, and here was fought one of the most brilliant and terrible battles of the war. For three days it raged with unexampled fury. At last the enemy, who had endured terrible losses, abandoned his invasion and retreated, closely pursued by his weary but triumphant adversary. In announcing this victory to the nation, Lincoln expressed a desire that on that day—the anniversary of National Independence—" He whose will, not ours, should ever be done be everywhere remembered and reverenced with profoundest gratitude."

The Union losses in this "most desperate" battle were 23,coo men killed, wounded, and missing; the enemy lost 14,000 men taken as prisoners alone. Costly as was this victory, it was productive of great results, for it proved to be the turning-point in the struggle.

The State of Pennsylvania subsequently purchased a piece of land adjoining the cemetery of the town—where some of the most determined fighting took place—to be used as a burial-ground for the heroic hearts who fell in this great and decisive battle. Lincoln was present at the dedication ceremony, held in November 1863, and delivered an oration which is entitled to take rank among the classics in literature. He said—

" Fourscore and seven years ago our fathers brought forth on this continent a new nation, conceived in liberty and dedicated to the proposition that all men are created equal. Now we are engaged in a great Civil War, testing whether that nation, or any nation so conceived and so dedicated, can long endure. We are met on a great battlefield of that war. We have come to dedicate a portion of that field as a final resting-place for those who here gave their lives that the nation might live.

"It is altogether fitting and proper that we should do this. But, in a larger sense, we cannot dedicate, we cannot consecrate, we cannot hallow this ground. The brave men, living and dead, who struggled here have consecrated it far above our poor power to add or detract. The world will little note nor long remember what we say here, but it can never forget what they did here. It is for us, the living, rather to be dedicated here to the great task remaining before us—that from these honoured dead we take increased devotion to that cause for which they gave the last full measure of devotion ; that we here highly resolve that those dead shall not have died in vain ; that this nation, under God, shall have a new birth of freedom ; and that government of the people, by the people, for the people, shall not perish from the earth."

The day of Gettysburg was further rendered memorable by the surrender of the city of

Vicksburg, the stronghold of the Mississippi River, to General Grant, with all the defences and an army of 30,000 men. Four days later, Port Hudson surrendered with 7000 men and 50 cannon.

The tide had turned at last, and was bearing the cause of freedom and right towards the shore in an ever-widening and deepening wave of triumph, resistless in its rush, momentous in its consequences.

CHAPTER IX.

FOR THIS END.

MEANWHILE Lincoln, with unwavering faith in the ultimate triumph of his cause, was preparing to consummate the grand object and aim of the war. He looked across the stricken fields, his gaze penetrated the battle-smoke, and beyond the war-clouds he saw his country once more at peace, free and united. Every victory brought the long-cherished end nearer ; every defeat drove it farther away.

His was not merely a policy of passive waiting. In the Cabinet he was no less active, no less strenuous than others in the field. He sent a recommendation to Congress to facilitate the passage of a resolution offering compensation to induce States to adopt the gradual abolition of slavery. The measure promptly became law, and that it had no immediate result detracts in no way from the merciful humanity of him who inspired it. Another practical step in the same direction soon followed, when an

5

Act was passed in Congress and approved by the President for emancipating slaves in the District of Columbia, and granting compensation to owners.

On the 22nd of September 1862, he issued his preliminary proclamation of Emancipation, declaring that on and after 1st January 1863 "all persons held as slaves within any State, or designated part of a State, the people whereof shall then be in rebellion against the United States, shall be then, thenceforward, and for ever free."

On the 1st of January 1863, the final proclamation of Emancipation was issued, though the war was not yet over. "I do order and declare"—thus reads this historic pronouncement —"that all persons held as slaves within the States of Arkansas, Texas, Mississippi, Alabama, Florida, Georgia, South Carolina, North Carolina, and certain portions of Louisiana and Virginia, are and henceforward shall be free."

To put the matter beyond all question, Lincoln supported a movement in Congress to abolish slavery by constitutional amendment, but he failed to carry the proposal. He did not, however, abandon it, and in his annual message the following year he urged the immediate passage of the measure. Accordingly, the "Thirteenth Amendment to the Federal Constitution" was proposed and adopted. By its provisions it became law that "neither slavery nor involuntary servitude, except as punishment for crime whereof the party shall have been duly convicted, shall exist within the United States or any place subject to their jurisdiction."

As the term of Lincoln's Presidency drew towards a close, the Democratic party set themselves to regain the position they had lost in 1860. There was no lack of material ready to hand that might be used in overthrowing their opponents. The war furnished a mine of grievances of all kinds. How slowly it was progressing; how enormous was the sacrifice of life in battle and campaign; how terrible to contemplate was the piling-up of the public debt. These and many more in the same connection answered admirably for a many-stringed whip wherewith to scourge the men who were striving to save the country and the nation from ruin.

Lincoln was, however, too well proven a servant of his country to be set aside at the bidding of an ambitious opponent or an envious faction. By an overwhelming majority the Union endorsed his self-denying and patriotic efforts to guide the ship of State amid the rocks and quicksands of internal strife and dissention. On the 4th of March 1865, he entered on his second term as President. His Inaugural Address is so masterly a summing-up of the whole political situation, that we cannot do better than reproduce it here.

"Fellow-countrymen," he said, "at this second appearing to take the oath of the Presidential office there is less occasion for an extended address than there was at first. On the occasion corresponding to this four years ago, all thoughts were anxiously directed to an impending Civil War. All dreaded it, all sought to avoid it. While the Inaugural Address was being delivered from this place devoted altogether to saving the Union without war, insurgent agents were in the city seeking to dissolve the Union and divide the effects by negotiation.

"Both parties deprecated war, but one of them would make war rather than let the nation survive, and the other would accept war rather than let it perish—and the war came. One-eighth of the whole population were coloured slaves, not distributed generally over the Union, but localised in the Southern part of it. These slaves constituted a peculiar and powerful interest. All knew that this interest was somehow the cause of the war. To strengthen, perpetuate, and extend this interest was the object for which the insurgents would rend the Union by war, while the Government claimed by right no more than to restrict the territorial enlargement of it.

"Neither party expected for the war the magnitude nor the duration which it has already attained. Neither anticipated that the cause of the conflict might cease when or even before the conflict itself should cease. Each looked for an easier issue and a result less fundamental and astounding. Both read the same Bible and pray to the same God, and each invokes His aid against the other. It may seem strange that men should ask a just God's assistance in wringing their bread from the sweat of other men's faces; but let us judge not, that we be not judged. The prayer of both could not be answered, and that of neither has been answered fully.

"The Almighty has His own purposes. 'Woe unto the world because of offences, for it must needs be that offences come, but woe to that man by whom the offence cometh.' If we shall suppose that American slavery is one of those offences which in the providence of God must needs come, but which, having continued through

His appointed time, He now wills to remove, and that He gives to both North and South this terrible war as the woe due to those by whom the offence came, shall we discern there any departure from those Divine attributes which those believers in a living God always ascribe to Him?

" Fondly do we hope, fervently do we pray, that this mighty scourge of war may speedily pass away. Yet if God wills that it continue till all the wealth piled by the bondsman's two hundred and fifty years of unrequited toil shall be sunk, and until every drop of blood drawn with the lash shall be paid by another drawn with the sword, as was said three thousand years ago, so still it must be said that 'the judgments of the Lord are true and righteous altogether.'

"With malice towards none, with charity for all, with firmness in the right as God gives us to see the right, let us strive on to finish the work we are in; to bind up the nation's wounds, to care for him who shall have borne the battle, and for his widow and his orphans; to do all which may achieve and cherish a just and a lasting peace among ourselves and with all nations."

Never before in the history of the country had any man been so completely regarded by the people as their "Father." All sorts and conditions, all ranks and classes came to him with their grievances, their troubles, their sorrows, their complaints. He received all alike; he helped, comforted, consoled, and re-dressed, "from the representatives from factions in Missouri to the old woman who applied to him to have a sum of money reserved from the wages of a clerk in one of the departments that he might pay her bill for board. Every man seemed to think that Lincoln could settle his little difficulty or provide for his little want whatever it might be."

The strain must have been terrific, but by no word did Lincoln give any indication of how heavily the long-continued responsibility, ex-citement, and anxiety weighed upon him. Already its indelible imprint was visible in face and features; but there was never a murmur, no one heard a word of weariness nor a wish for ease. He entered the White House strong and vigorous, with a frame of iron, and already he looked feeble, wan, worn and weary beyond the reach or the hope of rest. He used to say that he should leave Washington a better man if not a wiser for having learned what a very poor sort of a man he was.

"I have been driven many times to my

knees," he once declared, " by the overwhelming conviction that I had nowhere else to go. My own wisdom and that of all about me seemed insufficient for the day. I should be the most presumptuous blockhead on earth if I for one day thought that I could discharge the duties which have come upon me in this place without the aid and enlightenment of One who is wiser and stronger than all others."

At another time, in reply to a deputation that waited on him and spoke of the debt that the country owed him, he was quick to say—

" My friends, you owe me no gratitude for what I have done; and I, I may say, owe you no gratitude for what you have done, just as in a sense we owe no gratitude to the men who have fought our battles for us. I trust that this has all been for us a work of duty." Then he went on to say that the gratitude must be expressed to whom it was due—the Giver of all good.

It has often been said that Lincoln was not a religious man. How such a statement gained any currency is more than singular. It may certainly have arisen from his free Western ways—his story-telling, for example. His very reticence on the subject, which should have been sufficiently convincing, may have been misinterpreted; but there is not the slightest ground for thinking or even supposing that he was anything but deeply, indeed intensely, religious. There are numerous instances of it, and the following random extract, reading as it does almost like a confession of faith, is sufficient, even were it the only one, to finally dispose of a supposition as unworthy as ridiculous :—

"If it were not for my firm belief in an overruling Providence," he once declared, "it would be difficult for me, amidst such complication of affairs, to keep my reason on its seat. But I am confident the Almighty has His plans and will work them out; and whether we see it or not, they will be the wisest and best for us. I have always taken counsel of Him and referred to Him my plans, and have never adopted a course of proceeding without being assured, as far as I could be, by His approbation.

"To be sure He has not conformed to my desires, or else we should have been out of our trouble long ago. On the other hand, His will does not seem to agree with the wish of our enemies. He stands the Judge between us, and we ought to be willing to accept His decision.

We have reason to anticipate it will be favourable to us, for our cause is right."

In this spirit he went on from day to day, ever doing his duty as he saw it, ever striving to perfect it ; finding momentary release from the cares that so oppressed him in some humorous story, feeling more and more that he was an agent of a Higher Power rather than an independent actor in the great purpose that was being wrought out as the campaign went on. His cares were universal, as were his sorrows.

"The springs of life are wearing out, and I shall not last," he remarked on one occasion. On his shoulders he bore the weight of the nation and its future. Personal considerations troubled him but little; the ravages made by war in the ranks of his people were to him more matters for concern than that his life was threatened. The burden was enough to kill any man, and it was killing him. "I shall never be glad any more," he said. Still he kept working away, sad and weary, early and late, hoping, trusting, praying that all would be well.

"When it is over, my work will be done. I feel a presentiment I shall not outlast the rebellion," he remarked more than once; but never did his heart fail nor his energy slacken. He doubted not for a moment that strength would be given him for his needs, and, valiant in that faith, he kept to his duty, steady, bold, resolute, and without fear.

CHAPTER X.

ROUNDING UP.

THOUGH the proclamation of Liberation had been made, the war was not yet over; and though slavery had been abolished, there were still slaves in the land. The war went on, and seemed to be to all appearances as far from a conclusion as ever. In the beginning of 1863, the Union armies numbered nearly a million men, and were kept up to that strength till the end of the struggle. The military operations were of the most momentous importance, and on a scale truly colossal; and while there were disasters to deplore, the general results all pointed one way—that the end was in sight.

General Sherman drove the rebels under Johnston into Atlanta after a prolonged and desperate series of engagements, and laid siege to the city, which eventually surrendered. Then this brave and determined leader undertook an exploit as remarkable as any in the history of war. He decided to march to the sea through the heart of the rebel territory.

Leaving his supplies behind him, and cutting off all means of communication, he set out on this historic journey on the 12th of November. Though many efforts were made to stay his advance, he swept onward towards the Atlantic. The rebels were driven before him like leaves in an autumn gust, and he kept on with a precision almost machine-like. On the 14th of December Fort M'Allister was taken, and on the same day Savannah was occupied without difficulty.

After giving his men a brief rest, Sherman marched north, and on the 13th of January arrived on the confines of South Carolina. "They swept through the State like a very besom of destruction — tearing up railroads, burning bridges, living on the country, and attracting large numbers of negroes to them to learn they were free."

Pressing onward again, Columbia was reached, and the public property destroyed. Everything gave way before him. Several battles were fought, but the march was resistless, and Fayetteville in North Carolina was reached and occupied on the 12th of March.

Meanwhile General Grant was busily engaged in that series of actions known to history as the Battles of the Wilderness. Thousands and tens of thousands of brave men fell on both sides, but the rebel General Lee was gradually driven back. Grant gave him not a moment's rest, and by a series of brilliantly executed manœuvres drove him and his army into Richmond. Here was fought the decisive battle of the war. For three days it raged with unexampled fury and determination, and with ever-varying success. At length, on the 28th of March, after terrific fighting, victory crowned the right, and the rebellion was overthrown.

Great — indeed intense — interest had been aroused by the events which were happening round Richmond, for on the results depended momentous consequences. None was more deeply interested, none more eager for news, than the President. Leaving the anxieties and responsibilities of office behind, he went to see the fighting, and by great good fortune arrived in time to be present at the final act. As soon as victory was assured, he sent a message to the Secretary of State for War, announcing—"The triumphant success of our armies after three days of hard fighting, during which the forces on both sides displayed unsurpassed valour." The victory could not have been more complete—12,000 prisoners were taken, and 50 pieces of artillery fell into the hands of the victors.

Grant promptly went in pursuit of the flying enemy, and several battles were fought.

Lee, however, could not hope to withstand the determined onsets of the Northerners, and he was at length forced to surrender his whole army, which did not number more than 20,000 men, a fact which tells eloquently how desperate was the resistance and how heroic the victory.

The fall of Richmond decided the war, and was a signal for such an outburst of joy as never before had been known throughout the land. From mountain to mountain and from valley to valley the good news echoed: "Richmond has fallen: the war is at an end."

On the day after the surrender, Lincoln entered the town. There was no formal welcome, no display, nor, so far as he was concerned, was it the time for demonstration. But the poor downtrodden beings who had him to thank for their freedom got to know of his presence, and were not to be restrained. They seemed to lose all control of themselves when they heard that "Massa Linkum," as they called him, was in the town. "They sang, they danced, they prayed for blessings on his head." Crowds of them knelt weeping as he passed along. Never did king or conqueror receive such an outpouring of heart homage. "I bless de Lord that I have seen Massa Linkum," exclaimed one old negress, as he passed by where she was standing weeping the full tears of a heart grateful and joyous after long-pent misery.

"Glory to God! Glory! Glory!" shouted the black throng, as they tossed their hats and brightly coloured handkerchiefs into the air. Flags and streamers could not have made a braver show, would not have meant half as much, for it was spontaneous, it was the people's own expression of what they felt.

One old negro, the tears streaming down his face, exclaimed, "May de good Lord bless you, President Linkum!" and as he said so he took off his hat. Lincoln, his heart already too full for his eyes, lifted his hat in return, and passed on in silence amid crowds of kneeling and weeping people. In that supreme moment, in itself recompense sufficient for the labour of a lifetime, he remained outwardly calm and impassive; there was no light of triumph in his eye, no word of exultation on his lips. In his heart were gratitude and sorrow—gratitude to God who had enabled him to undertake and carry through so great a blessing to humanity; sorrow for those who had fallen, and sorrow of sorrows for those who mourned for them.

He returned to Washington deeply impressed with what he had seen, and busy with plans by which he hoped to heal the wounds that war had made, and bind together in a bond of love and patriotism all ranks and classes of his people, North as well as South, so that his beloved country might stand in the sight of the world united in all things as never before. Thus he thought, and so he would have laboured, but there was nothing more for him to do—though he knew it not, his work was done.

CHAPTER XI.

THE SAVIOUR OF HIS COUNTRY.

GREAT were the jubilations in the North over the return of peace and the triumph of right. The slave had been freed, and the blot that had so long defaced the flag of freedom was wiped out. The treasure in gold, and still more in blood, that had been poured forth was not thought in that hour to have been too costly a price to pay for so grand a consummation. Once more the country might proclaim her free institutions without fear and without shame.

And he who for four long years had borne the burden of war, who had to take the blame of reverses without sharing the credit of success, who had carried the weight of the responsibility for all that happened, and on whom the whole future of the country had rested, was rewarded by the grateful cheers of the whole people, and still more by the self-knowledge of having done his duty as he saw it, regardless of what men might think or say or do.

Times out of number he would gladly have given up the struggle and gone afar, where he might not hear the weeping widows and the crying orphans the war had made. Time and again would he have made peace had any mutual basis of peace been known; but there was none. To slave or not to slave was the question, and no other. Till that was settled he might not allay one jot of the suffering, the misery, the horror of war; he must endure to the end.

The war had not been to him a stepping-stone of ambition, but a stern duty, an inflexible national necessity, before which he could not but yield. At any time he would have accepted peace could he have freed the slave or even brought about the certainty of his future liberation. He was prepared to go to almost any length to gain this end: to see his country united once more he was ready to sacrifice himself.

It is well, perhaps, that none of the concessions he was willing to make were wholly acceptable to his adversaries, and that almost in spite of himself he had to risk everything to gain anything or, indeed, to save anything. By so doing he left nothing for future ages to accomplish or redeem, and for himself he achieved an immortality of fame, crowning by a martyr's death a life of honest labour, unflinching honour, and unswerving devotion to whatever was or seemed likely to be beneficial to his fellow-men.

Animated as he was naturally in no small degree by the spirit of conciliation, his whole thought now turned towards the future, eager to find some means of healing the wounds occasioned by the prolonged and frightful struggle. It was a noble ambition, and right nobly was he prepared to play his part.

The 14th of April 1865 was declared a public holiday in commemoration of the fall of Fort Sumter four years previously. Among the festivities was a special performance at Ford's Theatre, Washington; and by way of added attraction, it was announced that the President would be present. Nothing unusual occurred till about half-past ten, when there happened to be a brief interval.

Then all at once the half-hushed house was startled by the report of a pistol. Almost simultaneously a man was seen jumping from one of the boxes to the stage. For an instant he stood brandishing his weapon and shouting

" Sic semper tyrannis ! " Then he disappeared. The whole incident—so sudden, unexpected, and dramatic—took every one by surprise, and no one knew just what to make of it. Had it anything to do with the play ? each man asked his friend. What could it mean ?

Another moment and that question was answered. There was a commotion in the President's box, and as by magic the word passed round that he had been shot. The news could not be credited ; but it was indeed only too true : their good President, in the very hour of national rejoicing for peace restored, had been struck down and seriously, if not mortally, wounded. The assassin was an actor, John Wilkes Booth, who was actuated to his murderous deed by a desire to avenge the defeat of the Confederates.

Doctors were quickly summoned, but they could administer no aid that would preserve the fast ebbing life. All they could do was to ease any consciousness of pain ; but even that was unnecessary, for beyond deep and regular breathing Lincoln gave no other sign of life. Thus he remained throughout the night. Soon after seven o'clock the watchers by his side noticed a change in his appearance, and almost simultaneously the brave heart ceased to beat, and the heroic spirit sank to eternal rest.

By Lincoln's death the joy of the nation had been turned into mourning. "All was gloom," says a contemporary account. "Men walked in the public places and wept aloud as if they had been alone; women sat with children on the steps of houses wailing and sobbing. I saw in that day," adds the writer, "more of the human heart than in all the rest of my life. I saw in Philadelphia a great mob surging here and there between madness and grief, not knowing what to do. By common sympathy every family began to dress their houses in mourning and to hang black in all the public places. Before night the whole nation was shrouded in black."

Every possible honour was paid to the remains of the martyred President, and the whole civilised world joined with his fellow-countrymen in mourning his untimely fate. Few kings or emperors who ever lived have been so honoured in their hour of death as was this simple man of the people, elevated by his own genius and the votes of his fellow-citizens into equality with the most powerful sovereigns of the world.

His body was embalmed, and on the 22nd of

April was conveyed from Washington to its final resting-place in Illinois. All along the route were groups of people who had come to pay their last tribute of respect to " Honest Old Abe," as they affectionately called him ; and no man ever better deserved the honour and devotion of his people than he who, on the peril and at the cost of his own life, had saved his country and liberated a race.

" To all future time in America, the tall figure of Abraham Lincoln will stand out in heroic relief on the broad canvas of history, his head encircled with the aureole of martyrdom, second in the reverence of the people to none but George Washington."

Printed by
MORRISON & GIBB LIMITED
Edinburgh

THE "SPLENDID LIVES" SERIES—*Continued.*

FRANCES E. WILLARD.
The Story of a Noble Life.
By FLORENCE WITTS. Sixth Edition.

[*Twenty-fourth Thousand.*

FLORENCE NIGHTINGALE:
The Heroine of the Crimea.
By W. J. WINTLE. Eighth Edition.

[*Twenty-third Thousand.*

GARFIELD:
Farm-Boy, Soldier, and President.
By W. G. RUTHERFORD. Sixth Edition.

[*Twenty-third Thousand.*

JAMES GILMOUR AND THE MONGOL MISSION.
By Mrs. BRYSON, of Tientsin, China. Fifth Edition.

[*Twentieth Thousand.*

SIR SAMUEL BAKER:
His Life and Adventures.
By ALFRED E. LOMAX. Fifth Edition.

[*Eighteenth Thousand.*

PRESIDENT LINCOLN:
Plough-Boy, Statesman, Patriot.
By W. G. RUTHERFORD, Author of "The Story of Garfield." Fourth Edition. [*Sixteenth Thousand.*

JOHN HORDEN:
Missionary Bishop.
By Rev. A. R. BUCKLAND, M.A., Author of "The Heroic in Missions." Fourth Edition. [*Sixteenth Thousand.*

THE "SPLENDID LIVES" SERIES—*Continued.*

MARTIN LUTHER:
The Hero of the Reformation.
By E. VELVIN.   Fourth Edition.

[Fifteenth Thousand.

OLIVER CROMWELL:
The Hero of Puritan England.
By HORACE G. GROSER, Author of "The Kingdom of Manhood," etc.   Fourth Edition.

[Fourteenth Thousand.

JOHN BUNYAN:
The Glorious Dreamer.
By LINA ORMAN COOPER.   Third Edition.

[Sixteenth Thousand.

ROBERT RAIKES:
The Man who Founded the Sunday School.
By J. HENRY HARRIS, Author of "Robert Raikes: The Man and his Work."   Third Edition.

[Eleventh Thousand.

ALBERT THE GOOD (PRINCE CONSORT).
By W. J. WINTLE.   Third Edition.

[Tenth Thousand.

JOHN RUSKIN.
By R. E. PENGELLY.   Second Edition.

[Seventh Thousand.

JOHN HOWARD:
The Prisoner's Friend.
By LINA ORMAN COOPER, Author of "John Bunyan, the Glorious Dreamer."   Second Edition.

[Sixth Thousand.

57 AND 59 LUDGATE HILL, LONDON, E.C.

"*THE SPLENDID LIVES*" SERIES—*Continued.*

DR. J. L. PHILLIPS:
Missionary to the Children of India.

By W. J. WINTLE. [*Sixth Thousand.*

LORD SHAFTESBURY:
Peer and Philanthropist.

By R. ED. PENGELLY, Author of "John Ruskin."
Second Edition. [*Sixth Thousand.*

CATHERINE OF SIENA.
By FLORENCE WITTS, Author of "Frances Willard,"
etc. [*Sixth Thousand.*

HENRY A. STERN:
Missionary Traveller and Abyssinian Captive.

By E. C. DAWSON, M.A.(Oxon.). With Fourteen
Illustrations. [*Fourth Thousand.*

JOHN WESLEY:
The Hero of the Second Reformation.

By EDWARD MILLER, M.A.(Oxon.), Author of
"John Knox, the Hero of the Scottish Reformation."
With Portrait and Twelve Illustrations.
[*Third Thousand.*

ROBERT MOFFAT:
The Story of a Long Life in the South
African Mission Fields.

By HUBERT WILLIAMS. With Portraits and Illustrations. [*Third Thousand.*

*A Complete Catalogue of the Books published by the Sunday
School Union will be sent post free on receipt of a post card.*

www.ingramcontent.com/pod-product-compliance
Lightning Source LLC
Chambersburg PA
CBHW021412090426
42742CB00009B/1115